THROUGH THE EYES OF A CHILD

Through the Eyes of a Child

A Collection of Stories

THERESA CARTER

CarterPub

Edited by Kimberly Coghlan
Coghlan Professional Writing Services
www.coghlanwriting.com

Dedicated to the memory of Dorothy Carter and Linda Fleming. I will never
fill the hole in my heart created by your absence.

CONTENTS

DISCLAIMER

This book is a book of my memories—the way I saw things, first as a young child, then as I saw them after I reached the age where I accepted Christ as my *Lord* and Savior. I did my best to make it truthful, but people's perspectives vary, so other people in my life may have seen things differently than I did. This book is not intended to hurt or embarrass anyone, so if it causes any unintentional harm or embarrassment, please accept my apology. This book merely serves as a Christian self -help book intended to show readers the way I have handled my life's situations in an effort to help them to deal with similar circumstances.

| 1 |

INTRODUCTION

For God so loved the world, He gave his only begotten Son, that whosoever believeth in him should not perish, but have everlasting life.

~John 3:16~

We all start off in life with an earthly mother and father. They may not be married, and you may not live together as a family. Your family could be the most loving of all families that ever existed—or they could be the meanest and most uncaring of all families. Either way, we all start off with a mother and father, without exceptions. Those who are truly blessed, however, have a steadfast family, with a mother and father who love us unconditionally.

In families with multiple children, each child may see things differently. We may grow up in the same household with the same set of rules, and yet, we may turn out totally different because of the way we individually perceive our circumstances. Still, we all grow up viewing life *through the eyes of a child.*

Here's the kicker. After we begin to grow and mature, do we take it one step further? Do we take the most important step of all? Do we accept our Heavenly Father as our Lord and Savior? His guidance and our inheritance from Him are far more rewarding than anything our earthly father can offer, and with that assurance, we will always be someone's child—no matter the circumstances of our lives.

Our Heavenly Father is the most valuable of *all* fathers. He will see us through situations that we would not otherwise be able to face—even if we have the most loving earthly parents in the world. If we accept Him, we are His child, and *we still see Him through the eyes of a child.*

Life gets extremely tough. The devil just won't leave us alone, especially if we are on God's side. It's important to trust God to get us through those tough times. If we watch with childlike eyes and follow His steps, we can witness Him perform miracles that our earthly fathers cannot. God will keep us safe, even when we are facing the most trying time ever.

In trusting God, we know that one day, all will be well, and we will be with Him forever. God will protect us as long as we are in His will. That is not to say that trials will not come our way. They definitely will. A walk with Christ as our Lord and Savior is a difficult walk, but He will see us through it. Though God may discipline us for our sins, He does it for our own good.

In our daily walk with God, we must learn to lift each other up and forgive, for no one is perfect. We all need each other. We must pray for each other, as we never know what another person is going through since we all endure trials and tribulations that we do not share with others.

If we're lucky, we have many people who are important to us, but nearly everyone can identify someone who is a special part of our lives. Often, *you* may be the person who is special to someone else—even if you don't know it. Though people may affect us positively in our earthly lives, our eternal future is of upmost importance. Just imagine if the people we love have not given their lives to Jesus because they couldn't see Christ in us. What a tragedy! What a heartache!

I was lucky enough to have a very special person in my life who set an example of a loving, shining light—a person who let her light shine so I could see my Heavenly Father on Earth every time I saw her or talked to her. Oh, how I miss her! She took me under her wing and treated me like her daughter. She even said one time that if she had a daughter, she would want her to be like me—but not so shy. If she could only see me now. I'm not so shy anymore. She was my adopted mom, so to speak, and I was her adopted daughter—or that's what we called each other.

When she was close to going to her everlasting home, she told me she had listed me as her daughter in her funeral plans. "You better come to my funeral, and you better be sitting on the front seat with the rest of the family," she said. What a lump formed in my throat when she said that. She made my life so much easier because I saw God in everything she did. She used to say, "If you see anything good in me, it is of God—not of me."

I also had the very best biological mother in the world. She stood by me even when life was difficult for her, setting aside all her own hurts and hardships to see to it that I got everything I needed. She nurtured me and protected me from harm's way. I dedicate this book to my special mom and to my biological mother, both of whom nurtured me in the only way a true, loving mother could. They have both now gone on to be with the Lord, and I am anxiously awaiting to see them again and tell them once more how much they meant to me.

No matter how great my love for them was—and no matter how great their love for me was—God's love is even greater than both of them put together. That's the message I hope to convey in this book, which is a testament to some of the situations I have endured—circumstances to which you may relate.

I have learned to stand tall and stand strong, but most of all, to stand for Jesus. Even if we don't currently have an earthly mother or an earthly father in our lives, we have a Heavenly Father who is always there for us. He promises to never leave us or forsake us, and He promises to forgive us of everything if we only ask Him.

| 2 |

THE YOUNGER YEARS

But Jesus said, Suffer little children, and forbid them not, to come unto me: for of such is the kingdom of heaven.

~Matthew 19:14~

...and who knoweth whether thou art come to the kingdom for such a time as this?

~Esther 4:14~

On a freezing-cold, drizzly morning in February, I was born... a small, innocent child, totally unaware of what the cruel world had waiting for me. Had I known what was in store for me, Mama would have still been in labor because I would have refused to emerge. By the time I was born, Mama had over two hundred diapers hanging on the clothes line at one time, for I had three siblings who were also in diapers.

My earliest childhood memory consisted of being petrified to attend school at the young age of seven. I was fear-stricken by the fact that if I left for school, my mother would not be there to welcome me home when I returned that afternoon. That was an awful heavy burden for a scrawny seven-year-old to carry.

My father was a wife abuser, both physically and verbally. Never a day went by that he was not mistreating her. His father and mother had money and power in the small town I grew up in, so my father used this power. My father told my mother that if she left him, he would see to it that she would never see her beloved four children again, and I believed it would certainly happen that way. There was no doubt in my mind then—or even now.

At that young age, I decided my place in the world was to take care of my mother. I later learned that God has a plan for all of us. As a good friend and pastor of mine once said, "There comes a time in all of our lives to step up or step out."

I can remember my father slinging my frightened mother against our old yellow Rambler car early one morning after my brothers and sister had gone to school. She was trying desperately to get away from him and go to her parents' house for safety. I can still hear that awful sound that her small body made as she hit the car, just as I can see the terrified look on her face as tears rolled down her cheeks. With my young, frail body, I tried desperately to intervene, without any luck.

My mother always seemed tired from all the hard work she did while he was off somewhere fishing or having a good time. He wouldn't even let my mother go fishing with her father or spend time with her mother. My father would come home, demanding a hot supper and other chores from her. Still, with all she did, she always took time to set on the edge of her old, wooden bed, gripping her black, worn Bible and studying with all her heart, soul, and mind.

When she lay down for that short time at night, between dark and daylight hours, she knew she had God, and she could rest a little while without fear, but as the sun rose to begin a new day, the horror would begin all over again.

I knew I must always take care of her, for if she could take those cruel, uncalled-for beatings, day-in and day-out, to keep her children safe in her loving arms, then she deserved my total love and devotion 'til the day God chose to call her home to live with Him, safe, in His loving, merciful arms forever.

And so began the journey of my life, with many lessons of hardship —and God's undying love.

| 3 |

THE HEAT

They shall not hunger nor thirst, neither shall the heat nor sun smite them: for he that hath mercy on them shall lead them, even by the springs of water shall he guide them.

~Isiah 49:10~

Even a child is known by his doings, whether his work be pure, and whether it be right.

~Proverbs 20:11~

Heat is a word that has many meanings and connotations. There is the kind of heat you get from eating a hot pepper or the heat from an electric blanket as you snuggle under it to stay warm. A heater or a fireplace provides heat on a cold winter's night. And, of course, when people get furious, it is said that they are 'heated.'

I learned a hard lesson about heat as a young, curious child. That year, my grandmother's brother had given me a red and white Collie puppy. My uncle was a bachelor and had no children. I was his favorite niece, and so I named the puppy Whop after my uncle's nickname.

To stay warm, my mother was ironing in front of our fireplace, and she sprinkled water on the clothes, like most women in that day. The water helped remove wrinkles and made the ironing easier. When she ran out of water, she stepped into the kitchen to refill her cup, and I thought, *I'll help Mom out. She'll be so proud of me.*

I picked up the iron, but since I had no water, I licked the iron. Boy, was it hot! That day, I learned all about heat.

Mom put some baking soda on my tongue, and I didn't attempt to iron any more that day. As a matter of fact, I don't like ironing to this day.

But, just like God, my mother took care of me when I made my mistakes. God has done a lot of taking care of me, as it turned out. I'm always getting into something. You think a person would learn sooner or later, right?

| 4 |

THE HANDLE BARS

Wait on the Lord: be of good courage, and he shall strengthen thine heart: wait, I say, on the Lord.

~Psalm 27:14~

Mama worked hard for what little money she got. In fact, she worked harder than any other woman I have ever known. Nothing was ever given to her. She actually picked a bale of cotton the day one of my brothers was born.

I can remember when she and one of my brothers raised some hogs to make a little extra money for the family. They would load the hogs up when they were ready to be taken to the Bryan Brothers' company in another county. They worked hard, getting up early each and every morning so they could milk the cows and then feed the hogs. Some mornings, it was icy cold with snow and sleet, while other mornings, it would be blistering hot.

My brother loved playing the piano and the organ, and he practiced on an old piano that was ancient the day my grandmother received it. He wanted to save up to buy an organ of his own, and he though helping with the hogs would help him do just that.

When the time came to sell their hogs, they loaded them up in a rusty, worn-out trailer and drove to the other county with smiles wider than their faces. When they got there, they unloaded the hogs and received a check for their months of hard work.

The next day, they went to town and cashed their check, which, to them, was a lot of money. Then, they went to a small music store in the town where we lived. I stayed at home, and while they were gone, I decided to mix up some pepper sauce, hot sauce, and just a little ketchup for the baby chickens. I figured if they liked ketchup as much as I did, then surely the baby chicks would enjoy a treat. I mixed all this with some water and put it in the jar that the baby chicks drank water out of. I struggled to open the little latch on the small door, and all the baby chicks came running after their treat. Surprisingly enough, they drank it as if it was cold water.

None of them got sick, thank God, which reminds me of the Bible verse that says God protects the old and the young and the birds of the air. He sure protected my backside that day—and lots of days following that one.

When my mother and brother got home, I saw that they had bought an organ for my brother. It was sitting in the back of the truck as pretty as you please. At the time, I didn't realize that my brother had used his money to buy the organ, so instead of being excited and proud for him, I walked away, hurt. I knew mama loved music and just figured she loved him more because he also loved music and could play as well as he did.

After all, I had begged for a bicycle with a banana-split seat, and I figured if mama could afford an organ for my brother, then where was my bike? I was so upset. They went to town several days in a row to spend their money, and each time they came home, there was no bike.

Sometime later, when I had given up on the bike, Mama and my brother returned from another trip to town, and lo and behold, I saw the handle bars of a brand-new bike sticking up out of the back of the truck. The sun shone on it so that the brand-new handle bars were glistening in the sunlight. I was so excited. I tripped and nearly fell as I ran out to the truck to meet them, grinning from ear to ear.

My brother got the bike out of the truck for me, and it was the most beautiful bike I had ever seen. I was so happy. Of course, I probably wouldn't have got that bike if mama had known what I gave her chickens.

Looking back, I wish I hadn't been so selfish and that Mama would've spent that money on something for her, especially since she had so few things to call her own.

I'm not sure that I ever thanked Mama for that bike and the sacrifices she made for me. But like any good mom, she did it for me because she was just that kind of a mom. She loved me that much and knew what it meant to me.

I can still see the bike now. The purple bike had curved handle bars and a banana split seat, with a white glittery seat.

When I think about that story today, it reminds me of something important. If we, as God's children, could learn to be patient and wait on God, then we would see that the prize He has waiting for us at the end of our journey is more than worth waiting for. Too often, we rush ahead and try to do things our own way instead of waiting to see what God has planned for us.

| 5 |

DAVID AND GOLIATH

A man's heart deviseth his way; but the Lord directeth his steps.

~Proverbs 16:9~

I remember a time when I got into a with one of my brothers. Though I probably weighed a hundred pounds less than he did, I thought I was still strong enough to beat him. I had listened to the story about David and Goliath in Sunday school so I was confident I could win the battle.

Mom had gone to town to run some errands, so all of us kids were at home by ourselves, and my brother was in charge. I didn't like taking orders from him, and I got so mad, I pulled back my fist to hit him as hard as I could. Unfortunately, he lifted his glass of sweet tea at that precise moment, and I hit that instead.

A blue bump quickly arose on the end of one of my fingers, so I ran out to the old mule barn with a plan in mind. I'd make the injury look like an accident. I knew I'd be in trouble if Mom found out about the fight, so I had to hurry before she returned home. I climbed up into the hay loft, where I remembered some boards being loose. I lifted a loose board, placed my finger under it, and sat down on it as hard as I could.

Much to my dismay, the knot disappeared instead of getting bigger. So much for my big plans.

Of course, when mom got home, she uncovered the whole ordeal, and my brother and I both got into trouble. Thinking back to that day makes me chuckle, but over the years, I've realized that the situation mimics life. Sometimes, we plan for things to go a certain way, but God takes us in another direction.

Now that I'm older and wiser, I know that it's okay when plans don't turn out as expected because God has a better plan in mind.

| 6 |

THE SUGAR CANE PATCH

Therefore if any man be in Christ, he is a new creature: old things are passed away; behold, all things are become new.

~2 Corinthians 5:17~

After a hard day's work on the farm, our family would eat supper and sit down for a brief rest before going to bed. Farm days were hard work for everyone.

At one time, we had three families living in houses that my grandfather built on our farm, and we had a grocery room in our house—or that's what we called it back then. Once a month, my grandfather traveled to another town to buy groceries and tobacco products. We'd store the products in the grocery room, and the other families would retrieve what they needed. My grandmother wrote down the name of the product and the price of each item.

Then, at the end of the harvest season, they would "settle up." Granddaddy paid them what they had earned and gave Granddaddy money for the items they had purchased from him.

Grandma loved frying apple pies, and I remember her keeping a big bag of dried apples on a shelf in the grocery room. Those dried apples always looked so inviting to me, so one day, I got brave enough to climb up on that top shelf and help myself to them. Just like when sin looks so inviting to us, we just have to try one time. After one taste, I was hooked, and I kept going back for more. I had torn a small hole in the bag, just big enough for my small fingers to get through, and eating apples became a daily habit.

When Grandma noticed the hole, she thought a mouse had gotten into her dried apples, so she put out some mouse traps. And you know what? Grandma never did catch that mouse. If grandma was alive today, she'd probably still think it was a mouse eating her apples because I never revealed my secret.

Some years later, all the families moved off our farm and got places of their own, and we started growing sugar cane on the farm. Well, one night, my family and I were sitting around the fire chewing some sugar cane when all of a sudden, we heard a truck rumble to a stop down the road next to our cane patch. My brothers and I ran out on the porch to see who it was, but the truck took off, so we went back inside and commenced our snacking.

A few minutes later, the dogs started barking, so we stepped back out on the porch to investigate, and we heard the sound of sugar cane popping. Someone was stealing our cane! One of my brothers ran into the house, grabbed his shotgun, and fired a shot up in the air. In the dark night, we heard people running and shouting in the cane field.

The next day at school, I sat by one of the girls whose family had lived on our farm. Noticing scrapes on her legs, I asked, "Where'd you get them scratches?"

She laughed and said, "Well... uh..."

"You don't have to tell me," I said, interrupting her. "I already know."

I still get a chuckle thinking about her and her family running through the briar patch just like Br'er Rabbit in the children's fairy tale.

The story reminds me of sin, though sin isn't funny. However, thanks to Jesus, we can repent, and our sins are washed away.

| 7 |

IF THAT ISN'T LOVE

As one whom his mother comforteth, so will I comfort you; and you shall be comforted in Jerusalem.

~Isaiah 66:13~

Then spake the woman whose the living child was unto the king, for her bowels yearned upon her son, and she said, O my lord, give her the living child, and in no wise slay it. But the other said, Let it be neither mine nor thine, but divide it.

~1 Kings 3:26~

Early one frosty morning, I was feeding the cows, and I discovered a sick calf that had diarrhea, or what we called the scours.

After telling my mother about the sick calf, I had to go to the barn and get the medicine, which was very dangerous to people. I knew we had to be careful when giving the calf the shot. When I returned, I climbed over the fence and straddled the calf to administer the shot. My mother was on the other side of the fence, holding the calf by its ears. Unfortunately, the other calves had been sucking on this calf's ears, which was normal for younger calves. As such, the calf's ears were slippery, and as I moved to stick the needle into the calf's shoulder, the calf jumped back, and my mother lost her grip.

Before I realized what happened, the needle slipped, and the tip stuck my finger.

"Oh, Lord," my mother yelled. Tears poured down her face. "Gimme the needle," she wailed.

"Why you want the needle?" I asked.

"It's my fault. I lost my grip and made you slip. If you're gonna die, then I'm gonna die with you."

"I ain't gonna die," I yelled stubbornly. I put the needle in my pocket. Then, I picked up a stick and stabbed it in the place where the needle pierced me. "I'll just make sure all the medicine comes out with this blood."

"Give me the needle now," my mother ordered.

"No, Mama," I argued. "Look? I'm fine. I'm just sick to my stomach, but that's because you're making me so upset. If you stick yourself, and you die, and I live, then I'll feel horrible," I said as tears formed in my eyes.

Well, I didn't die that day, but I often think about how my mother said she'd want to die if I passed. I was lucky to have a mother who loved me so much—and as much as my mom loved me, God loves me more. It's difficult to fathom a love so boundless.

Over the years, when friends have betrayed me or when I feel lonely, I remind myself of God's love. God loved me so much, He sent his Son to die for me.

| 8 |

THE SKUNK

And now why tarriest thou? arise, and be baptized, and wash away thy sins, calling on the name of the Lord.

Acts 22:16

I have a niece who has grown up to be a beautiful young woman with two beautiful children of her own, which is strange because I remember her as a baby.

When she was young, she was so small—and quiet as a church mouse. I recall one hot, sticky summer day when she accompanied me to our old cow barn to give a baby calf a bottle of milk. My niece wanted to tote the bottle all by herself, and truth be known, the bottle probably weighed as much as she did. Still, I let her carry the bottle, and I laughed as she struggled and dropped the bottle several times.

Finally, we reached the barn, and I shut the door behind us so the calf couldn't run out. My niece reached the bottle out to the calf, who immediately started sucking away. Though the calf was snatching it every which a way, my niece hung on to that bottle as if her life depended on it.

All of a sudden, one of our dogs that had followed us into the barn started barking at something behind an old feed bin.

"Oh, hush," I scolded the dog. "It's just one of the cats."

The dog's barks only escalated, and once again, I yelled at the dog to be quiet, but the dog's yelps only grew louder.

"Old Mute, leave that cat alone!" I screamed it this time. Just then, I saw a small black nose stick out from behind the bin. "It's just a mouse," I told the dog, who continued to bark. I glanced over at my niece, who kept feeding the calf, ignoring the commotion.

When I looked back at the bin, a big black skunk darted out, it's fluffy tail high in the air. As frightened as I was, the dog must've been even more scared because it quit barking and ran toward me. I tried to get my niece's attention while the dog cowered behind me.

My niece still wasn't paying attention, so I yelled, "Run, run."

She stood up and lumbered over to me, looking confused. Before any of us could get out of the barn, the skunk raised its tail and aimed. The spray came out like a water hose, but the flow turned into a mist as it flew through the air. Surprisingly, the odor didn't smell the same as when a skunk gets run over on the road. Instead, the odor produced a hot, burning sensation in my nose, throat, and lungs.

When I finally made it back to the house, I saw my mother standing at the kitchen sink. The screen door slammed when I entered the house, and Mama said, "A skunk just ran by the kitchen window."

"It sure did," I replied. "After spraying us."

Though I didn't think it was funny, Mama laughed between instructions. "Go get in the tub. You'll have to soak for a while and then scrub real hard. And you'll hafta burn your clothes," she said.

You know, that old sunk stench is a lot like sin. It stinks, and it's hard to wash away. In fact, we *can't* wash it away—not by ourselves. Only God wash away the stains of sin.

| 9 |

THE RECIPE

For I know the thoughts that I think toward you, saith the Lord, thoughts of peace, and not of evil, to give you an expected end.

~Jeremiah 29:11~

There are many devices in a man's heart; nevertheless the counsel of the Lord, that shall stand.

~Proverbs 19:21~

Jesus answered and said unto him, What I do thou knowest not now, but thou shalt know hereafter.

~John 13:7~

For my thoughts are not your thoughts, neither are your ways my ways, saith the Lord.

~Isaiah 55:8~

What do you think about when you hear the word recipe? If you are my age, then you might think about the Baldwin's recipe on *The*

Waltons. For you younger people, *The Waltons* is a television show that aired in the 70s. Or perhaps you think about your mama's good ole homemade recipe for chicken soup she made for you when you were sick. When I hear the word recipe, I think about both.

As a young adult, I raised calves to make a little extra money. Truth be told, I was trying to make a *lot* of extra money. I started buying baby Holstein calves from a man. If you know anything about Holsteins, then you know that they are all black and white. They all look just alike.

Well, I had gotten up to forty baby calves, and I'd get up at the crack of dawn, just like the mailman— whether rain, sleet or shine—to begin the long, hard chore of feeding the calves. They always seemed to be starving and always ran to me. They were all in a small lot (pen) together. I had to feed them a bottle of powdered milk twice a day, so as soon as I finished that first feeding, it would be time to start all over again.

Since all of them looked alike, I had the bright idea to go purchase a box of magic markers. Every day, I placed a mark on the calves' faces to identify the one that I had just fed, and I used a different color marker each day. By the end of the week, I couldn't see the calves' eyes for the marks I had placed on their faces with the magic markers.

One calf cost me one hundred dollars. Then, I would put another one hundred dollars in their powdered milk. Finally, I had to spend another hundred dollars in feed to get them up to approximately three hundred to four hundred pounds. Not to mention the cost of the magic markers.

Just as I was settling into this little project of mine, my calves started to die. I had bought the calves when they were just a day old, just after they got their first milk. A baby calf must get some of its mother's milk as soon as it's born, or it will not survive, but my cows lived until they were nearly full size. As it turned out, the man I bought the calves from had gone up north and purchased some new cows that were sick, unbeknownst to him. They had a disease called BVD, which affects cows when they reach the weight of 300 to 400 pounds.

You can imagine my frustration when I went out to feed them and found two or three dead cows each morning. After all, I had $300 to $400 in them—and a lot of hard work—and once again, not to mention my magic markers. I remember being so angry, I'd kick the dead calf.

I frantically researched the situation, looking for a solution to my problem. I was ready to try anything. In fact, I actually fixed one calf some chicken soup, which didn't work, by the way. The cow died, anyway.

As I searched for a solution, I came upon a man who told me that it might help if I gave the cows a little whiskey. I was desperate, so I thought I'd give it a try. And, even though he instructed me to give them a little whiskey, I thought, *If a little would help, then a lot would help a lot more—and a lot quicker.*

I didn't even know how to buy whiskey, but the man offered to buy me some, so after he brought me the bottle, I got started on my new recipe. I mixed a little powdered milk with a *pint* of whiskey and fed it to my calves.

Unfortunately, the man's tip didn't work, and my calves continued dying. But I'd like to think they died with a smile on their faces.

That's when I decided that I needed a new career, and at the time, I wasn't happy about it one bit. I was hurt an angry.

Looking back now, it's hilarious that I got my cows drunk. And I also realized that raising cattle wasn't in God's plan for me. Had I continued raising calves for a living, I'd be too old to do that now, so I wouldn't have had a retirement plan or much social security to live on.

Years later, I found a new career. God had been whispering in my ear for a long time that He wanted me in prison to do His work. To be honest, I often wondered if God meant that I'd be spreading the good news as a convict. Luckily, that wasn't the case, and I worked as a prison employee.

So, here's to the cows and their whiskey.

| 10 |

REMEMBER WHEN

And now abideth faith, hope, charity, these three; but the greatest of these is charity.

1 Corinthians 13:12, 13

Then they that feared the Lord spake often one to another: and the Lord hearkened, and heard it, and a book of remembrance was written before him for them that feared the Lord, and that thought upon his name. And they shall be mine, saith the Lord of hosts, in that day when I make up my jewels; and I will spare them, as a man spareth his own son that serveth him.

Malachi 3:16-17

I'll never forget a visit to PaBill and MaCiles house. They were my grandparents (my mother's parents). We called them. On this particular night, we were supposed to have supper with them, which was a real treat—especially for my mother since Dad rarely let us enjoy visits with them. My mother had spent all afternoon making my favorite casserole. I just knew it was going to be mouth-watering good.

My uncle, my mother's brother, lived in that old white wooden house with my grandparents. He had a lot of junk scattered everywhere

—including all sorts of items lying in the yard, even some old farm equipment.

It was already beginning to get dark when we arrived because Mama had to milk our cows first, which was how we supplemented our income. As we got out of the car, mother handed me the casserole to carry inside. I was so proud of being chosen to do that task for her. Even back then, my mom was so special to me. I wanted to please her in every way I could.

Well, I got out of the car and started towards the house carrying the perfect casserole dish, and leave to me, I tripped on some sort of farm equipment, and I fell. I didn't even worry about catching myself with my hands as I hit the ground. I just hung on to that casserole for dear life because I didn't want to disappoint my mama.

Before my mother could say anything, I shouted, "I didn't drop it!"

Mama rushed over to me, cooing, "Oh baby, I'm not worried about the casserole. Are you okay?"

I can still see the look in Mama's eyes. I was so worried about that casserole, but she was only concerned about me. That was love, and Jesus loves us the same way—even more so. He loves us more than any brother, sister, mother, father, or friend can.

If we try to love Him back—and even if we don't—He is there for us. He loves and cares so deeply for us, and He is constantly watching out for us.

I'm a lot older these days, but I still fall down—both physically, mentally, and even spiritually. And sometimes, when I fall or feel let down, I can feel God saying the same sweet words my mama used. "Are you okay?"

I never wanted to disappoint Mama, but I was also so anxious to earn Daddy's approval. One day, he told me to accompany him to a small town near the place where we lived—to the tractor supply store. I was so excited that he asked me to go.

I remember being on the back seat of that small maroon and white car we owned at that time. It was just him and me, and I was beaming with pride. When we arrived at our destination, he told me to stay in the car, and he got out and went inside.

When he returned to the car, he was holding a piece of welded iron from a tractor part he was trying to fix. He opened the back door, handed it to me, and told me to hold it and not lay it down on the floor of the car.

I had no idea that the piece had been welded, and I certainly didn't realize that it was still hot from the process. I grabbed it and immediately realized that it was hot—really hot. Regardless, I held on to that piece of iron.

At that point, Daddy had gotten into the car, and my hand was melting into that piece of iron. I could even smell my flesh burning. In an effort to please my father—and not to get into trouble, I hung on to that hot piece of iron all the way home.

When we arrived home, my father got out of the car, and without a word, he reached for the piece of iron and walked off towards the tractor shed. Of course, he knew where to grab it so it wouldn't burn him—something he had unfortunately failed to tell me.

Anyway, fighting back the tears, I got out of the car and went into the house. My aunt, my father's sister, was visiting from another state. At the time, we were living with my father's parents, and my aunt had come to visit them. So when I came in holding my hand, she immediately rushed over to me.

"What's wrong? Let me see your hand," she said.

I was so upset, I couldn't reply, but she immediately started first aid. She was so gentle and so caring that day, which felt good—inside *and* out.

My hand eventually healed, and the kindness she showed me that day remained in my heart forever. And I never stopped trying to get Daddy's approval. If we all tried to win our Heavenly Father's approval as much as I tried to appease my earthly father, I know He would certainly be happy, and we would certainly be blessed.

I was fortunate enough to have two aunts who loved me unconditionally. After my father passed away, my mother and I would go to my aunt's house, her sister. I was very close to my aunt. She would always welcome us with board games and simple card games. She fixed us snacks and meals. I can still taste those rice crispy treats, cheese and crackers, and sandwiches. They were so good, and I always seemed to be so hungry, but looking back, I honestly believe I was just hungry for someone to love me and my mom.

My mama and my aunt have gone to heaven, but today, I'm still hungry—hungry for God's love. Sometimes, when I'm in the truck by myself, I can feel His presence so close, it brings tears to my eyes. I know that I don't deserve God, but He is always there.

| 11 |

LOOKING BACK

And the rains descended, and the floods came, and the winds blew, and beat upon that house; and it fell not: for it was founded upon a rock.

~Matthew 7:25~

One night, I was lying in bed trying to go to sleep, and I had so many thoughts running through my head that sleep was impossible. Suddenly, I recalled a moment when I was in the ninth grade. It was the first time that I looked up to another person other than my mother.

My ninth grade English teacher. She was a very kind person. I had such a great time in her class, and English remained my favorite subject throughout my college years.

I was so attached to her that it was hard to leave her room and go on to another class. Then, in the twelfth grade, I had another English teacher who was also special to me.

As I grew up, the distance between me and those special teachers also grew. And it broke my heart. I didn't know it at the time, but the Lord was making me stronger with each heartbreak. In my college years, I, once again, became attached to my English teacher, and I'll never forget that I made a 98 in her class as a final grade. And it wasn't that I was especially smart. No. I simply learned to care for her, and that made me strive to do my very best in her class.

Looking back, I think that maybe each of those special teachers was a mother figure to me. I just know that I had experienced a lot of hurt in my life, and it was good to connect with someone who cared about me.

After I finished college, God brought a wonderful friend into my life, and I was on top of the world. When I lost her to cancer, the world collapsed around me. I could hardly go on. The hurt was so unbearable. It took months to get over losing her. Truth be told, I'm not over the loss yet—and I probably won't ever fully recover from it.

I realize, however, that God knows best. For thirty-something years, she brought out the best in me. Someone once told me that it takes time to stop hurting, but I don't think I'll ever get enough time behind me to heal completely.

When I was really depressed, a good friend of mine told me that the only thing that helped him was to stay busy and try to be happy with what he had. I resolved to move on, but then, four years later, my mom passed. Once again, I had to depend on God to get me through the pain.

Now, I know that each trial God takes me through is for my own good. It makes me stronger and helps me be able to face the next one. God allows storms in our lives to see what we are made of and to make the next time bearable for us. He makes us stronger, step by step, instead of throwing everything at us at once.

Our lives are built upon the rock, or they are built upon sand. If we fail at one trial, then next time, we must learn to build our lives on the rock. Everything God *says* is for a reason, and everything God *does* is for a reason, and everything God allows to happen to us is for a reason.

| **12** |

MY SUPER HEROS

(Mentors)

My little children, let us not love in word or in tongue, but in deed and in truth.

~1 John 3:18~

If you have read the beginning of this book, then you've come to realize who had the most profound impacts on my life—my best friend, who had a loving and kind personality and was concerned about my spiritual welfare—and my mother, who was always concerned about my physical well-being.

Throughout the years of my life, many people have meant so much to me. They have influenced my life's decisions and helped guide me in the right direction. I often think of another good friend of mine. She was a nurse and worked at the same facility I did. You could tell by the way she carried herself that she was a Christian and that she loved her job. She cared for the people she treated. It was not just a show to her—and not just a job, either.

And, of course, when I think of people who have influenced my life, I can't forget my aunt. I remember once when we were discussing the fact that neither of us had left anything to be remembered by. At the time, I was thinking too literally because now I know that we *have* left something behind.

She left behind the love of her family, and she influenced me by showing her compassion for me. I will always remember her kindness. She would listen to me without judgment and lead me to make the right decisions without forcing them on me.

Someone once said that the greatest legacy we can leave someone is our character. This is so true. If we let our spiritual light shine, then people have something to remember—and something to pattern their lives after.

So, as I think back to all the people who have influenced me, I can only hope that I have inspired others as well.

| 13 |

RIGHT ON TIME

My times are in thy hands

~Psalm 31:15~

Right when I had become complacent with the way things were in my life, getting accustomed to the pain, the disillusions, and the hurt that we all face in our lifetime, along came Jesus—right on time.

In an effort to search for the love that was missing in our family, my older sister became pregnant out of wedlock, but Jesus turned this tragedy into a blessing like He has with so many tragedies in our lives.

She had a beautiful baby boy. Had it been a girl, my dad would've probably put my sister and her beautiful child out of our home and into the street to face life on their own. But Jesus knew that a baby boy was just what we all needed to pull our family together.

My father grew to love this child with all his heart, and my nephew, with the help of God, became one of, if not the *most* talented people I have ever known. Among his many talents was music.

Low and behold, when my nephew was seven, the person who would become my very best friend showed up at our church to perform a special program with the children. She spotted my nephew, and with the help of a precious member of the church, she saw the talent God had given him. She took him under her loving wing and used his God-given talent to bless our family.

She had a gospel group with a member of our church, and she made him part of the group. She spent endless hours working with him. She even had him playing the keyboard with her group when he was still only seven. She also had him singing some songs with the group and some by himself.

And guess what? The love my father had for this child drew him into the church. Sure, it began only as a way to see my nephew perform. When Daddy started going to church, I prayed that, eventually, he would give his life to Christ.

I, too, began to feel God's presence in my life more and more. Isn't God great! Because of my nephew, I'm convinced that my father was blessed with the gift of salvation. My sister was blessed with a child to love—and a place to stay and rear my nephew. Also, my mom was blessed with a place to enjoy going instead of being beaten or verbally abused all the time. My nephew was blessed with talent and a way to develop it, with the love from a special person. And me? Wow. I was blessed with the greatest of all earthly friends one could ever hope for or deserve.

What an abundance of blessings for one family—and all because God sent this wonderful earthly angel into our lives and this beautiful boy child!

God puts certain people in our lives for a reason, but sometimes, we need to stop and listen to God's call for us to help and support each other—to work for Him.

Thinking about this situation helps me because, like all of us, I struggle to always remember that Jesus has His own timing for everything. I often need to be reminded that Jesus is always and forevermore on time.

| 14 |

TO ERR IS HUMAN, TO FORGIVE, DIVINE

Forbearing one another, and forgiving one another, if any man have a quarrel against any: even as Christ forgave you, so also do ye.

~Colossians 3:13~

And be ye kind one to another, tenderhearted, forgiving one another, even as God for Christ's sake hath forgiven you.

~Ephesians 4:32~

If a trial gives us patience, then I must be the most patient person the world has ever seen.

After my friend began treating my nephew as her own son, she took me as her own daughter, and my love for her grew tremendously. She let God use her to bless us, and she was the most wonderful person I have ever known, 'til this day, except for my mother.

Our families ate meals together. We played games together. She bought all my clothes—and beautiful clothes, they were. Our families became as one. Eventually, I went to her church and became a part of her church family. We even spent every Christmas Eve together.

I can remember one particular Christmas when I had to work. Times were hard then, for my father had passed away, and I was responsible for my mother's bills like lights, water, and medicine, which was only fair because I lived with her. I had bills that had to be taken care of also. Mother had a small social security check, but it was tied up in something else.

While I was at work on that Christmas, Mama called me at my job.

"Hey, honey, guess who's here?"

My friend and some people from the church had come and delivered Christmas gifts for us. I was frustrated because I couldn't afford Christmas gifts, and trying to justify not giving them gifts, I told Mama, "Mama, I couldn't afford to get any extra gifts. Oh well, she probably just got me some stupid ol' clothes, anyway."

"I didn't know that my mom had passed the phone to my friend until I heard her always-happy voice. "Hey, there! How are you?"

I was mortified, but she never once mentioned what I said. Of course, I never got any more clothes, though. And despite me putting my foot in my mouth, our friendship grew even more beautiful and stronger.

On another Christmas, I remember buying her a cell phone. But just as soon as I made that purchase, the devil began to work on me, putting thoughts into my head. "You bought her a phone, and she won't even call you."

After that, I didn't even give her a chance not to call me. I was always calling her. But then, the devil gave me those bad thoughts again, and I decided to test our friendship. One day, I resolved *not* to call her until she called me.

Three years passed by, when she didn't call me, and I didn't call her. Thinking back, I was so stubborn and full of pride. I was so wrong. The whole situation hurt me, and I'm sure it hurt her.

Just when I had begun to settle into the fact that our friendship just wasn't meant to be anymore, there came Jesus—right on time. I drove passed their old country church, and at that time, I was attending another church. They had just ended their old-fashioned Sunday-night service. The sun was beginning to go down for the night, and the sky was so beautiful.

As I drove by, I saw her standing outside telling everyone good-night. I can still see in my mind's eye the white outfit that she had on as she stood there with the sun radiating about her.

In that instance, God began to deal with me once again. God spoke to me. "Call her. Call her," God urged through a voice in my head.

I became very upset. "No, Lord. She hasn't called me, so why should I call her? If she truly loved me, she'd call me."

That voice kept nagging me, and the next night, I yelled, "Okay. I give up!"

I picked up my phone and texted her— 'Are you guys okay?'

Then, I chunked my phone toward the bed, but it was in midair when it started ringing. That ring seemed to echo through the room. I scrambled toward the phone to answer it.

"Hello," I said.

I heard sobs on the other end of the receiver. "I have cancer," she wailed.

I'll never forget that moment and how my gut wrenched with sorrow.

As you know, there are no redoes in life, but we were able to start over, and we became closer than we ever were before.

I see now that God is continuously giving us second chances—even when we don't deserve them. There is no greater love than His. And I learned a very important lesson from this situation—never take the people you love for granted. One day, they'll be gone, and all you'll have left is the memories.

| 15 |

MY MILLION DOLLARS AND MY MANSION

In my father's house there are many mansions; if it were not so, I would have told you. I go to prepare a place for you.

~John 14:2~

Several years ago, I became a millionaire. It was all by chance and only for a very few minutes. At the time, I was a shy female in a man's world. I had just begun what I called my first real job—in a prison.

That day, I decided I needed a snack, so off to the facility canteen I went. After much deliberation, I decided on a pack of peanut M&M's, and I went back to my post, where I set down and opened the package. To my surprise, I found that all the M&M's were white. My first thought was that they had just forgotten to put the coloring on them. Then I thought, *Hmmmm. These M&M's are coconut flavored.* I detest coconut, so I threw the whole pack in the garbage.

Approximately, two days later, I was at home watching my favorite show on the tv when I saw a M&M's commercial. My mouth flew open when I heard that if you open a package of all-white M&M's, then you win a million dollars.

Well, like they say… "Easy come, easy go."

All my co-workers insisted that they would have gone to the dump and hunted the package. To this day, when I think about it, I don't feel so good.

Still, I've come to terms with it. What is a million dollars when I have a Heavenly Father who is richer than anyone I know? It will all be mine one day. I'll probably die a poor woman with little money, but still, one day, I'll be rich.

| 16 |

WHAT A DAY

Casting all your care upon him; for he careth for you. Be sober, be vigilant; because your adversary the devil, as a roaring lion, walketh about, seeking whom he may devour:

~1 Peter 5: 7-8~

Submit yourselves therefore to God. Resist the devil, and he will flee from you.

~James 4:7~

I've heard it put, 'Your karma is what you do to me, and my karma is how I *react* to what you do to me.' But then again, karma is not a Christian word. Still, I've also heard the saying, 'What goes around, comes around,' and I think there's some truth in these mantras.

I remember one long day at work that began with me sitting at the computer. I had my back turned toward the door, and I heard the door open, but I never turned around to see who was entering.

It turned out to be one of my co-workers, and let's just say our chemistry just did *not* mix. We had worked together for many years, and no matter how much we both tried, we just could *not* get along.

Well, as she entered the room, she announced in a loud voice, "Good morning. Why are you not speaking to me?"

"I didn't even see you come in. My back was turned," I explained.

"Whatever," she said, and she stormed out of the room, slamming the door.

Another officer was sitting in the room with me, and he hadn't spoken to her either, but she didn't say anything to him.

After I finished my work on the computer, I stepped into my co-worker's office and asked for the key to the mailroom to do the inmate mail. She merely grunted and handed me the key.

I proceeded to go open the mailroom, and when I came back into her office to give her the key back, she said, "What is wrong with you?"

I glanced at two other officers who were also in her office. "Do you mind giving us a little privacy?" I asked.

After the other officers left, I lost my cool. She had some underlying issues that I won't mention, but of course, I had my own issues as well.

I respected this co-worker for her knowledge in the field, but I could never understand why she couldn't be nice.

After that instance, I drew a little cross on my wrist with the blood of Jesus dripping off it when I was at work. I figured if I was covered in His blood, then nothing could harm me. I also wrote a Bible verse on a small piece of paper and cuffed it in my hand anytime I was around her.

I don't know if that co-worker ever received karma for her unpleasantness, but I do know that *I* am only responsible for what I do. God knows I've made my share of mistakes, and I've had my share of being punished by God, but all we can do is strive to be Christlike and ask forgiveness when we fall short.

| 17 |

THE FINAL GOODBYE

To everything there is a season, and a time to every purpose under the heaven: A time to be born, and a time to die; a time to plant, and a time to pluck up that which is planted; A time to kill, and a time to heal; a time to break down, and a time to build up; A time to weep, and a time to laugh; a time to mourn, and a time to dance; A time to cast away stones, and a time to gather stones together,; a time to embrace, and a time to refrain from embracing; A time to get, and a time to lose; a time to keep, and a time to cast away; A time to rend, and a time to sew; a time to keep silence, and a time to speak; A time to love, and a time to hate; a time of war, and a time of peace.

~Ecclesiastes 3:1-8~

There comes a time in each of our lives when we will say goodbye for the last time to someone special. We never think about it until that time comes, and we may not even know that it's the last time to say goodbye. Regardless, when we lose someone special, we're left heart-broken, maybe even stunned, but most assuredly, speechless.

God had allowed me to see my earthly angel quite often in her final days, and I will be eternally grateful To Him for that. Still, it's never enough time. Close to the end, I stood by her bedside, and I was heart-broken to see her in such pain—and not only physical pain, but the pain knowing that she was leaving her loving family.

She was a devoted mother, a devoted wife, a devoted friend, and a devoted Christian, if ever there was one. She knew that one day she would see the people she loved again, but even on her death bed, she was concerned about them. Would they be okay without her?

During her life, my friend showed me that she loved me by her actions and with letters and cards she sent to me. But I'll never forget the last time she showed me she loved me—the time she verbalized it before going to heaven.

As I bent over to hug her, I noticed that as weak as she was, she held me so tight, I could feel her cheek bone press into my cheek. She was so frail from the disease. I didn't know it at the time, but she was saying goodbye to me for the last time.

As I was walking away from her bedside that day, I heard her call out the words, "I love you."

I immediately stopped in my tracks and slowly turned around. I was completely at a loss for words. She had never spoken those words out loud to me, even though I knew she loved me from all our special ways of communicating.

I finally managed to say, "You know I love you, too." Saying it out loud made it sound so awkward.

I walked away with tears in my eyes, still not knowing that that would be the last time she would ever speak to me.

I visited her again later in the hospital, but at that time, she wasn't able to communicate anymore. The last time I saw her in the hospital, I was sitting on the small couch in her hospital room. Her husband and son had stepped out of the room for a second, and all of a sudden, I noticed her struggling to open her ever-so-weak eyes. It seemed to take forever, but she managed to open one eye. Immediately, the other eye opened ever-so slightly.

She looked straight at me, and a tear rolled down my cheek. She then closed her eyes. I could remember my grandmother doing the same thing. And later on, my mother. At that point, I knew that it was close to time for her to exit this world—and to be with the God that she worshiped and adored with all her heart.

I am sure she is in heaven now, singing and playing the piano for the One she held so dear. I also know, without a shadow of a doubt, that she is there waiting for me.

When I get sad about her being gone, I think back to one time when I went to her house to take her some food after she had gotten so sick. I was trying to talk her into eating, so I told her, "Let's have a picnic."

"I'm not eating," she said, ever-so boldly. "We'll have a picnic under the tree of life one day."

That makes me smile because I know she is waiting there for me, and I can't wait to see her. So, when the good Lord calls me home, we'll definitely be having a picnic.

| 18 |

THE CROSS IN THE SKY

Blessed are the poor in spirit: for theirs is the kingdom of heaven. Blessed are they that morn: for they shall be comforted.

~Matthew 5: 1-2~

On August 29th, 2017, I received the text that I had been dreading most—the one that was the worst of a lifetime. It was news that my dearest friend had passed on to be with the Lord.

I got up and dressed, as usual, for the day's work. I was a private person, so I pretended it was just another day, though my heart was breaking. Just as I was exiting the door, my mother asked, "How's your friend?"

"She's dead," I replied glumly.

Mother had never asked me that before, so I wasn't sure if she had already heard the news. But I did know that my mother, along with some other family members, resented the fact that I spent so much time with my friend.

At that moment, I thought, '*You can be happy now. I'm all yours again.*

"She's better off," my mother responded casually.

Wordlessly, I stormed out of the house, but my brain reeled with thoughts. *How can people say such a thing? Maybe she is better off, but I'm not—I am not better without her.*

The pain was so deep, I cried all the way to work, and when I arrived in the parking lot, I could go no further. I just could not bring myself to get out of the truck. So, I took a deep breath and called my boss, who was understanding.

I told her my plan to go to Jackson, where my nephew lived at the time. I had his house keys, and he would be at work so I could be by myself there. My boss even agreed to let my mother know where I'd be.

I just knew I had to be by myself because, in my mind, no one could identify with my pain. On the drive, I reeled against God.

"Please see me through the pain," I prayed. "Or are you going to ignore me again?" I asked. "For years, I prayed that you'd heal her, and you didn't!"

As I neared Jackson, my sorrow nearly overcame me, and I could barely see to drive with tears streaming down my face.

"God, please," I cried out. "Please show me a sign that she's okay—and a sign that I'll make it through this!"

At that moment, I looked up into the dark night sky, and low and behold, I spotted a cross lit up in the sky.

I later found out that the cross was on top of a tower, and it was lit up with white Christmas lights, but I saw that cross at exactly the right moment, and that was all I needed to make it through the rest of the day. It was indeed *my* sign.

When I finally made it to my destination, I got out of the truck, fumbled with the keys, and entered the house. Inside, I broke down and wept—wept with grief, with frustration—and with relief for my sign. I didn't know what to do next, but suddenly, I recalled a situation in which a cousin of mine had lost his wife while she was pregnant. He was so heartbroken, he got in a hot shower and cried for hours.

So that's what I did. I got in the shower and turned on the hot water—*only* the hot water. I stayed in there until all the hot water was gone, and once it had time to reheat itself, I started the process all over again.

Thanks to God's grace, mercy, and love, I made it through that day and many a difficult day since then, though there is not a day yet that I don't shed a tear for the loss of my friend, who so blessed our lives.

I learned a lot that day. God was there for me, even when I was angry and hurt and yelling at Him for not doing what *I* wanted. I learned that God can still use a broken vessel. Now, when I get to feeling down and missing my friend, I close my eyes and picture that beautiful cross shining out from the dark night. Indeed, it was my sign, and I know that one day, my friend and I will be reunited, and oh, what a glorious day that will be.

| 19 |

JUST STAND STILL

Be still, and know that I am God: I will be exalted among the heathen, I will be exalted in the earth.

~Psalm 46:10~

We've all experienced it at one time or another—a crossroads—a time when our hearts are pulling us in two different directions. Which way do we go? What road should we take?

Well, if you're anything like me, you'll *over* think the decision, but when it boils down to it, you probably already have a plan in mind, and you're just trying to convince yourself that what you want is the right choice.

But here's the thing: it may very well be the *wrong* direction. So take it from me—someone who is a bit older with more experience—someone who has experienced multiple crossroads—someone who has made some good decisions—and some very bad ones.

When you find yourself at a Crossroads, don't make an immediate decision. Instead, pray about it. Read and study the Bible. Ask your friends for advice. Though you may be trying to discern God's will, it's important to remember that God does not always shout. Sometimes—

well, most of the time, He just whispers. It is easy to ignore a whisper, so you have to be conscientious of the signs that God may show you.

Perhaps it is a Bible verse that keeps coming to mind. If so, that is no coincidence. It may be a memory of the way you were taught somewhere down the line. Whatever the case, just stand still and listen to what your Heavenly Father has to say.

Stand still, and don't make a decision until you know that God is speaking to you, and once you realize what God is telling you, don't ignore Him. Do as he says, for that is the only way to be happy.

Like the old folks used to say, 'Don't put the cart before the horse.'

| 20 |

JESUS MEANS ALL THE WORLD TO ME

For God so loved the world, that he gave his only begotten Son, that whosoever believeth in him should not perish, but have everlasting life.

~John 3:16~

Like many others, my road to salvation was rocky at times. I remember, at the age of twelve, when my pastor's wife approached me while we were having a revival at our small country church. She said she'd like to talk to me and my sister. I agreed to meet with her, but I knew what she wanted to talk to me about, so I beat her to the draw and walked the aisle of the church that night.

Of course, I knew all about religion because I had grown up with it. Even though my mother had to milk the cows every morning, my mother made sure we were always in church. So, I knew all about God, and I had also become good at avoiding trouble. Still, God had not yet become my master.

Then, at the age of thirty-two, God convicted me while I was lying in bed one night. God spoke to me loud and clear, and it was one of the longest nights of my life. He told me I was on my way to hell. Of course, I argued with Him.

"Hey. I joined the church when I was twelve," I maintained.

Well, we know who won that argument, right? And thank God He did!

God spoke to me clearly. "To some, I come more than once, and to others, I only come one time. I am coming to you one time. If you do not accept me now, I will not come again."

Well, that isn't right, I thought, as I tossed and turned all night. There was absolutely no sleep for me, and the still, quietness of the night was deafening to my ears. *What will I tell my friend who thinks I'm saved? What's my father going to say? For years, he has harped on not being embarrassed in public. Getting saved at my age would be so embarrassing—embarrassing to my family, my friends—and for me. After all, I've been in church since I was a child.*

Well, morning finally came, and I had not decided to accept Jesus as my master, though He was still tugging at my heart strings. We were having a revival during that time, and they were baptizing that day, so I decided to slip a change of clothes in the truck behind the seat—just in case I decided to turn my life completely over to Jesus.

I can still remember the exact seat where I sat—down to the color of the seat covers and the color of the carpet. All during the sermon, the words, "One call, that's all," rang through my head. When the song, *Just as I Am,* which seemed to be the longest hymn in history, began to play for the benediction, I stepped one foot out into the aisle. That one foot felt as heavy as ten feet, even heavier.

In that moment, I decided to turn my life completely over to him—to trust and obey, just as I was. It wasn't the sermon that saved me that day, for I didn't hear a word of it. And the act of walking down the aisle didn't save me. No, it was God tugging at my heart—and me turning my life completely over to Him.

'Till this day, that one step is all I can remember. God carried me the rest of the way. From that moment on, I was not alone anymore. God was there, and He still is with me today. He is my strength, my guide, and my best friend. Jesus means all the world to me.

You really don't start living until you get Jesus on your side. But guess what? Times only got harder for me after that. Before, the devil had me, so he left me alone, and now he doesn't have me, so he tempts me each and every day. Sometimes I pass the test, and sometimes I fail. But guess what? Jesus is always ready to forgive me, and He is always there for me, even when friends and family are not.

Isn't God great? Today, I look back and thank Him for what He has done for me and the places from where He has delivered me. Where would I be without Him?

| 21 |

CAN'T GET RIGHT

The Lord also will be a refuge for the oppressed, a refuge in times of trouble. And they that know thy name will put their trust in thee: for thou, Lord, hast not forsaken them that seek thee.

~Psalm 9:9-10~

Have you ever been to that point in your life where no matter what you do, it just doesn't seem to turn out the right way? I've been there, myself.

I have a 'friend' who says that we are a product of our work environment. Well, that may be so, but what did that mean for me? After all, I worked in a jail.

Over the years, I got to know many inmates, and I definitely realized that most inmates were victims of their circumstances in life. Very rarely had I met an inmate who had no redeeming qualities about them at all.

I remember five specific offenders that I was working with and how each one affected me. I was positive that one of them was saved, and I was pretty confident that the others were, too. These five offenders often bowed their heads to ask for the blessing before they ate, and in fact, if I forgot to do this myself, some of them had absolutely no problem reminding me that I needed to do the same.

I nicknamed on of these guys, 'Can't Get Right.' He was very knowledgeable on so many subjects, and once, he told me that he had read the whole Bible many times. This man was very kindhearted, and I came to realize that he was a victim of his rearing—and of life itself. If his background had been different, I don't think he would've even been in prison.

This man was always respectful to everyone, and I knew he would've done anything for me, including standing by me in the toughest of times—even if it meant hard times would befall him. He could've been a well-known artist, an athlete, or anything his heart desired, but for some reason, he just couldn't get it right.

And you know what? I can relate to 'Can't Get Right.' Life is hard, and at times, I feel like I just can't get it right, either. But I refuse to give up. I've heard my nephew say the phrase, 'A setback to come back,' which is so true. With each trial I endure, I know I will come back even stronger.

We're all like 'Can't Get Right,' so instead of judging others, it's better to share God's promise of grace because when everything seems hopeless, God will see us through our trials.

| 22 |

THE SILVER TONGUE DEVIL

(CHOICES)

But he that knew not, and did commit things worthy of stripes, shall be beaten with few stripes, For unto whomsoever much is given, of him shall be much required: and to whom men have committed much, of him they will ask the more.

~Luke 12:48~

So then every one of us shall give account of himself to God.

~Romans 14:12~

Neither is there any creature that is not manifest in his sight: but all things are naked and opened unto the eyes of him with whom we have to do.

~Hebrews 4:13~

Be sober, be vigilant; because your adversary the devil, as a roaring lion, walketh about, seeking whom he may devour.

~1 Peter 5:8~

Over the years, I've thought a lot about the what-ifs in life—and the choices we make. When it boils down to it, our choices show how dedicated we are to serving the risen Savior—the one who hung on that cruel wooden cross, just for us. If we truly considered God's sacrifice for us, would we make the right choice?

I've come to realize that the more a person understands and the more authority a person has, the more they will be expected to do God's will. Simply put, the greater the *power,* the greater the responsibility—and the greater the *knowledge,* the greater the responsibility!

We must take responsibility for our own actions and make a conscious decision to allow God and others to help us accomplish what is right in God's eyes and what we know to be right in our hearts. No sin is hidden from God—none!

Imagine being in a classroom, taking a test. The teacher walks out of the room, and you just happen to look up and see your best friend cheating. Would you confront your friend? Would you tell the teacher? Or would you simply ignore the situation in hopes that it would go away?

Have you ever picked up a pen at work and taken it home with you? Maybe it was by accident, and you didn't even discover it until you got home. Do you go to the trouble of taking it back the next day? Sure, it is a small item, and true, they may never miss it. Still, we know it is wrong, and as simple as it seems, it is still stealing.

Imagine being in the midst of a group of sophisticated people. You don't want to be left out of the cool bunch, but what if they are talking negatively about someone you care about—or even someone you don't know. Do you take up for that person, or do you ride with the crowd and say nothing—or maybe even join in?

What if a group of friends were laughing about Jesus or the church? Would you deny Jesus, or would you stand up for Him? We all hope that we would stand up for Him.

I read that J. C. Penny lived like a Christian but actually did not get saved until he was admitted to a sanitarium later on in life. It is said that he was seventy years old before he joined a church. One time, he almost lost his business because he wouldn't bribe a chef in a nearby hotel with a bottle of bourbon once a week. It is also said that he tithed at least 10% to 30%. And if we don't tithe 10%, are we stealing from God?

Imagine your best friend doing something morally wrong and being ostracized for it by a larger group of people. Would you go with the crowd and condemn your friend? Or would you continue to welcome your friend in your home with open arms, knowing it was only a mistake—that your friend is only human and truly sorry for the action. Would you ask your friend to come dine with you, knowing others will condemn you, too, for your association with the friend? What if you and your family are the only ones that still love and trust this person? And would it change anything if you could see into the future, knowing that your friend would betray you later on, down life's road? Would you still stand by your friend? And what if this person keeps making the same mistake over and over again, even after apologizing? Do you keep forgiving your friend?

What if a store gives you too much change, but you don't realize it until you get in the parking lot? You may be in a hurry to get home because you have company coming for supper. Do you take the time to return the change to the cashier, or do you just hurry home, knowing no one will be the wiser?

Life is complicated, and sometimes the choices seem simple, but at other times, the 'right' choice is more convoluted. When you do make the wrong choice, God forgives you if you truly repent and are truly sorry. He also forgets, once we repent.

Whether it is a small sin or a large sin, it is still a sin. And sometimes, the hardest action is forgiving ourselves for the mistakes we've made. Sometimes, it seems impossible to move on. Sometimes, it seems impossible to forgive. Sometimes, it seems that life just gets too hard to bear, but you have to keep on living. If you are still here on this Earth, then God has a plan for you.

Always pray when making small decisions *and* big decisions so you will make the right choice. I often try to understand why people do things that hurt other people—especially since I know that I am just as capable of making big mistakes and sinning as the next person. For me, I feel like each time I sin, I'm just driving the nail in Christ's hand a little deeper.

As I said, life is hard, and though things aren't always black and white, God is always steady, always there, and always faithful. It's essential to include God in our choices to get through this journey we call life.

| 23 |

THE BOTTLES

Rejoice evermore. Pray without ceasing. In every thing give thanks: for this is the will of God in Christ Jesus concerning you.
~1 Thessalonians 5:16-18~

As I've said before, there are no redoes in life. Once you make a decision and carry through with it, it's a done deal. That makes me think of a decision I had to make.

From the time I was little, I always had a desire to take care of my precious mother. When my mother was eighty-seven years old, I was sixty-one, and I wasn't confident that I could support my mother financially. I had a decision to make—one that I was so nervous about, but with God's help, I made the right choice, and I was able to be with my precious mother 'till the day she passed.

But making the right choice isn't always that easy. I've been through a lot of grief in my life, and I remember a time when I was bogged down with heartache. As part of my self-therapy, I walked up and down my road every chance I had. Sometimes, I even walked seven miles a day.

One day, I decided to write a prayer down and place it in a bottle— to have a written account of my prayer. After that, each day, I took a prayer in a bottle with me on my walk and threw it into the creek below my house. I'd watch the bottle swirl in the water for a while. Then I'd get down on my knees, looking up to the heavens and repeating the prayer, in hopes that God would show me His mercy and answer my prayers quickly.

I returned every afternoon to see if the bottle was gone, maybe in hopes that God reached down his merciful hands and retrieved the bottle to answer my prayer. Logically, I knew that God didn't have to reach down and retrieve that bottle, just like I understood that God knew my prayer even before the bottle hit the water—or even before it left my lips.

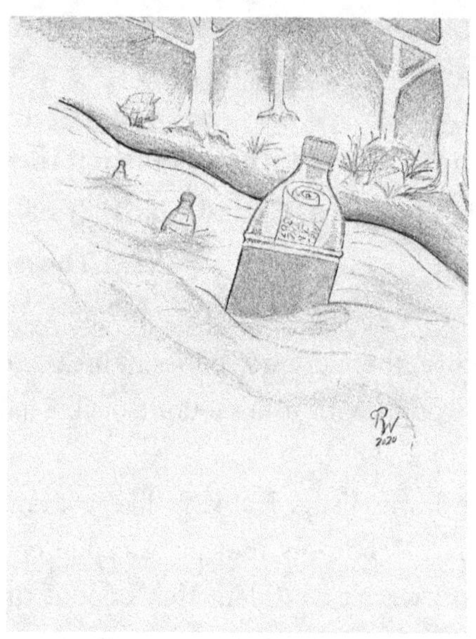

However, to my dismay, the bottle would be gone every time I returned to the place where I threw it in, but the prayer would not be answered—or so I thought. I did this for weeks. Then, one day, out of shear desperation, I gave up. What was the use?

I still continued my walks, as that seemed to be the only time I could be by myself and regain any composure to continue to face the hard road of life. Then, one day, several weeks later, I returned to the creek, and low and behold, I spotted one of my bottles.

Seeing that bottle gave me renewed confidence because I was sure that God had finally answered one of my prayers. I reached out to retrieve the bottle, but I couldn't reach it. I was too old to get closer to the water's edge, and it was much too dangerous.

And you know what? I never figured out what prayer was in that particular bottle, and I'm still not sure which of my prayers God answered. But over the years, I've learned not to rush God—and not to test Him.

God doesn't always give me the answer I want, but He always answers in his time. Today, I still continue my walks and my prayers, but I've come to accept that God will do what he sees best for me, which is not always necessarily what I think I want.

I still have so much pain, and one day, while standing at the creek, I looked for a bottle, and seeing none, I briefly thought about jumping into the water—to end my life, to stop the pain. But God wouldn't let that thought linger too long because I realized that God has something yet for me to do.

We're all in this life together—and it's not easy, not for any of us. But take it from me, if you are still here on Earth, God has something for you to do. He will get you through the pain—or at least help you to bear it, if only one step at a time. And even when all seems lost, God is walking with you—with every step you take.

| 24 |

TODAY I BURIED MY HEART

For the Lord himself shall descend from heaven with a shout, with the
voice of the archangel, and with the trump of God: and the dead in Christ shall rise first:

~1 Thessalonians 4:10~

I retired four months before my precious mother went on to be with the Lord. It seemed like she became ill the moment I retired.

Mama had made several trips to the hospital before we decided to place her in hospice care. She so desperately wanted to spend her last hours at home with her family. Because of the COVID-19 pandemic, we couldn't stay with her when she went in the hospital, so she hated being without her family during the hospital stays.

Five days after Mama was placed on hospice, she drew her last breath here on this place we so often call home. I was devastated. The very next day, I buried my heart when I buried my mom. I had so many ifs and so many regrets. Why did I do this? And why did I do that?

It was a difficult time for me, but I learned to look at her passing differently. As soon as she drew her last breath here on Earth, she went to a new home—a better home—a place with no pain and no sorrow.

She went to be with her mama and father, her brother and sister. I know that she is waiting to see me, also.

I loved her so much, and that hasn't changed. And now, I must carry on her legacy and do what she would want, even though she is not with me. Oh, how I look forward to the day when I can see her once more.

Still, the pain of loss never truly leaves us, but when I'm feeling especially sad, I praise God for the time He gave me with her. I indeed buried my heart the day I buried my mom, but I *will* see her again!!!

| 25 |

A TRIBUTE TO MOTHER'S DAY

In loving memory of the two people that I most cherished in this world—the one that raised me, loved me, and kept me safe—and the one that showed me the way to Jesus. May we soon meet again.

And God shall wipe away all tears from their eyes; and there shall be no more death, neither sorrow, nor crying, neither shall there be any more pain; for the former things are passed away.

~Revelation 21: 4~

My flesh and my heart faileth; but God is the strength of my heart, and my portion forever.

~Psalm 73:26~

I fondly recall one bright sunny day, late in the afternoon, just about supper time, when I was sitting in the swing on the front porch. Our pastor had made us two swings that looked just alike—one swing for each end of the porch. They were beautiful swings with hearts craved out on the back of both of them. They were also varnished to a beautiful shine.

Well, on that particular day, I was sitting in one of the swings, and my dear, sweet mother was sitting in the other one. We were waiting for our company, our dearest of all friends, to arrive for supper. As we sat there waiting, we were watching the hummingbirds and all God's other great creatures.

All of a sudden, I heard a car driving up the road, and I looked up. They had arrived! I was so excited. I was always happy to see them, but this particular day seemed different, somehow.

Everyone's faces were smiling, and we all were reaching out to hug one another with Christian love, as we always did. Just as I reached them, with my mother beside me, I felt a warm, salty tear run down my cheek. I couldn't figure out what was going on, but I was *so* happy to see them.

Suddenly, I opened my eyes, and my pillow was soaked with tears. It was just a dream—a beautiful, wonderful dream. But as the splendor of that dream faded, I looked around and saw complete darkness. And a deep loneliness overcame me. The air had a chill to it, even though it was warm inside the house. I hugged myself, as the house seemed so empty, for I was the only one there.

I've had many cold nights like this—and many a wet pillow. They say that dreams like this are part of the grieving process, but I've often wondered when the grieving stops and when I'll be able to move on with my life without feeling the void of people I've loved.

I've learned to place one foot in front of the other because, in my heart, I know that my grieving will never actually come to an end. Will there ever be another day filled with complete joy—where the pang of grief doesn't affect me? I don't have the answer to that question, but I do know that one wonderful, glorious day, we will meet again. One day, there will be no more pain and no more death. On that day, all my questions will be answered. On that day, we will walk hand in hand in a beautiful place, past the crystal river and underneath the beautiful tree of life.

Grief is universal—something we'll all experience at one point or another. But those of us who know God can stand on faith that one day, grief will be extinguished. So, if you should see my loved ones before I do, please let them know that I'm okay and that I am on my way.

| 26 |

A PARABLE

A PARABLE: THE SOWER

MATTHEW 13:1-23, MARK 4: 1-20, LUKE 8:4-15

They have sown wheat, but shall reap thorns: they have put themselves to pain, but shall not profit: and they shall be ashamed of your revenues because of the fierce anger of the Lord.

Jeremiah 12:13

Often, I find myself watching television evangelists, though I'm not too impressed with these preachers because they always ask for so much money. Even though I know it takes money to support their cause, I wonder if their 'cause' is just to fill their pocketbooks.

However, one particular day, I was listening to a TV evangelist's sermon about sowing seeds. After his message, he challenged his listeners to write a check for the Lord's work and write in the bottom left-hand corner what they would like to receive—and then mail the checks to him.

Now, trying to outsmart this man, I wrote a check for the Lord's work, but I didn't make it out to him. As a matter of fact, I wrote two checks that day, with two different wishes on them, and I sent the checks to causes I deemed worthy of God's work. Now I knew I was testing God, and I also realized that my wishes probably wouldn't come true, so I only made the checks out for $25 apiece. No sense in spending a lot of money on a wish that wouldn't come true.

Then, lo and behold, two days later, a mutt showed up at my house. Yep, one of the items I wished for was a puppy. But this wasn't the puppy for which I had hoped. To be honest, it was the ugliest dog I have ever seen, so I gently nudged the dog with my foot and said, "Go on home. You can't stay here."

In response, the dog just stared at me—and followed me around wherever I went. No amount of shoving or screaming would convince that ugly old dog to get away from me.

Several days passed, and I finally gave up. That dog just wasn't going anywhere. My wish had been answered, and I got a new dog. However, my new dog wasn't that smart. In fact, he wasn't bright at all.

For example, he had chased a car going down the road, and he didn't see or hear a car coming up behind him, so he never got out of the road, and the car behind him hit him. Being the hard-headed dog he was, he fought for his life and won the battle. However, after that, he continued to limp on one leg.

Then, several weeks later, we placed an electric fence up to keep the raccoons out of our watermelon patch. My dog was crossing the fence when he realized that it was hot. Instead of going straight through the fence, the dog decided, in mid-journey, to turn around and come back out. Well, needless to say, he got tangled up in it. Luckily, he got loose before I could even unplug the fence, but several days later, he was walking around the fence again. This time, he remembered that the fence had hurt him, so he decided to smell it instead of trying to jump through it.

When his nose touched the fence, it zapped him, and he got so frazzled, he forgot which leg was his good leg. So, he went running down the road that day, hopping on his bad foot. Bless his heart. He never got any smarter.

As it turned out, I named that do Twenty-Five, the amount I had written on the check, as a reminder not to test the Lord. For me, that was a lesson learned—'Be careful what you ask for, and also, you get what you pay for.'

Trust me. If I ever write a check like that with my wish for God on it again, the check will be a bigger amount. I'll also pray about it a little harder and ask God's will to be done.

And if you're wondering about the second check with the other wish on it... well, let's just say that story turned out worse than my tale of Twenty-Five, the unattractive, unintelligent dog.

| 27 |

MY PRAYER TO YOU, SWEET JESUS

Our Father, which art in heaven,

Hallowed be thy Name.

Thy will be done in earth,

As it is in heaven.

Give us this day our daily bread.

And forgive us our debts,

As we forgive our debtors.

And lead us not into temptation, but deliver us from evil.

For thine is the kingdom, and the power and the glory, forever.

Amen

Matthew 6:9-13

My dear, sweet Savior and best friend, I am coming to you on bended knees and with a burdened heart. I am asking you to forgive me of all my wicked sins. I do not deserve your forgiveness; this, I know. I asked, on the day of accountability, that I not be judged by you with a fair trial but that I be judged by you with mercy. I am unworthy to stand before you, but I bow on my knees, worshiping you with all my heart. At times, I have sinned with eyes wide open, knowing you were speaking to me, and I openly disobeyed you. At other times, I made mistakes.

I can never deserve your love or the price you paid for my sins. I can only imagine the heaviness of that old wooden cross that you carried for me. The big splinters that drove in your back as you struggled to carry it. The blood that flowed down your back as you did so. The sins you bore for me were even heavier. I know also that I am just as guilty as the men who crucified you that day. Each time I sin, I feel that I drive those big carpenter's nails deeper into your loving hands. I am sorry for the shame you had to bear that day when they ripped your clothes from your body.

You did it all for me. I know that I am human, and I know I will continue to sin each and every day. I ask that you often remind me where you brought me from and where I would be this day if it were not for you and your undying love for me, the ultimate price you paid for my sins. I ask that you send me a strong hand to guide and teach me.

I ask that you find a place that you would like for me to serve you by serving others. I can never deserve or repay what I owe to you but know that I have a willing heart to obey. You, alone, can give me the strength to trust and obey—to follow in your holy steps as much as humanly possible.

I look forward to the day when I will be reunited with the saints that I knew here on Earth—the ones you so kindly loaned to me to make my life more of a joy than I could ever deserve. But most of all, I look forward to being with you—to be close to you—to be made more like you in each and every way.

Jesus, I pray that you come back soon. Today would not be too soon for me. But 'till then, dear Jesus, help me to always be aware of the temptations put before me. Help me to always realize that the devil knows exactly what formula to put together to win us over to his side. He knows who to put in my life and what circumstances to put in front of me to tempt me in my weakest moments.

Help me to be able to always see the way I should travel, in your footsteps. It is kind of like when I was a child. Sometimes, I would struggle to step in my mother's footsteps as she walked in the yard. They seemed so far apart. I know that I can never walk always in yours, but I will do my best. Should I fail, bring me back.

I know that I must pay for my sins, just like any good parent disciplines their child. Help me to accept my punishment and to learn from it. For I know deep in my heart that you have already taken the ultimate punishment for me.

Dear Jesus, please know that I am willing to serve you in any way, but I will need your strength to do so. I, however, do not feel worthy to teach others, for I have fallen short so many times myself. Although I may know the Bible and what it says and believe every word of it, I probably am the most sinful of all. I think, though, that I am more than qualified to reach out to the elderly, the sick, and the down-hearted because I have plenty of experience in that category. It takes little effort to pick up a phone and ask someone how they are feeling. It takes little effort to pick up a card and send it to someone. It takes little effort to cook a meal for someone who is in need.

I understand that you do not call the qualified, but qualify the called. I look forward to you giving me the tools I need to serve you. I can look back and see times I have passed a person on the highway asking for assistance. Someone standing in the doorway of a store asking for spare change. It was not my place to judge if that person actually needed help. To say to myself, 'There are jobs out there; go get one.' I have one. It is, however, my place to ask myself this question: 'Is that actually God, and am I passing Him by? Or am I passing by an opportunity to serve you?'

How many times do we walk past someone like that? I know the Bible teaches us to visit those in prison. To help those who are in need or sick. It states that if I have done it to the least of these, then I have done it for you.

Help me be the kind of servant that does this for you. Help me to serve you by serving others.

| 28 |

THOUGH NONE GO WITH ME

THOUGH NONE GO WITH ME

(Through it all)

"A man that hath friends must shew himself friendly: and there is a friend that sticketh closer than a brother."

Proverbs 18:24

In your lifetime, you will meet, if God blesses you, someone special. Perhaps it will be one true friend—a person who is faithful, loving, and devoted to you. If you're blessed with a friendship like this, then that person will stand by you no matter what—despite your faults, your shortcomings, your status in life, or your monetary riches—or the lack thereof.

Over the years, research has taught us a lot about what sustains a true friendship. A true friend pushes you to be your best. Friends are people who have chosen you to build a close-knit relationship with and enjoy spending time with you. Your minds and souls bond together to make a strong, meaningful, and lasting relationship. Friendships are based on trust between each other, and once that trust is gone… sadly, so often is that friendship.

You can only be in that type of relationship with a limited number of people. We, as humans, are only able to focus on and devote a limited number of hours to make a friendship work… because it does take both parties working to keep a friendship striving.

More often than not, a true friend is willing to put your happiness in front of the friendship itself. Friendship is also built on respect for each other. Friendship makes life so much richer and the hurts and disappointments that we face so much fewer. As one person put it, it's like finding a four-leaf clover—something hard to find—but something you're lucky to have.

There is so much difference between a real friend and someone who is just friendly. A person who is just friendly is simply a person who is nice or kindhearted. Maybe you get to feeling down, and a friendly person comes up to you and listens to you. Maybe they are just being polite. Maybe they just happen to be in the right place at the right time. Let's just say they are willing to spend time with you at their own convenience and not go out of the way to spend time with you. They don't actually even have to like you. That is kind, but that trait is not a relationship.

God has blessed me throughout my lifetime. God has sent many people to help me with the struggles in my life. The hurt in my life has been numerous—and so deep, but none of us have a monopoly on pain. It comes in all sizes and in all forms and at all times throughout our lives. But as a believer, we have to stand on the fact that *through it all,* God gives us *what* we need and *when* we need it every step of the way.

Years ago, I had some serious health problems. I was constantly sick and had even visited the ER five times. Finally, a doctor prescribed me some medicine to help my condition, but lo and behold, my insurance didn't cover the medication, which was very expensive. Being from a small town, I guess word got out that I as having trouble, and guess what? I received $500 from a business—a meat processing plant, no less. I still think about that, to this day. Somewhere, a person was behind that donation—a person who represents what Christianity is all about—being the hands and feet of Jesus for people in times of need.

So, yes, God has used His people to be there for me, when I needed Him most. God also sent me a friend whose love for Christ—and for me—was endless and remarkable. I know she is in heaven at this very moment, with my mom. I am confident they're having a great time, though they both wanted to stay here on Earth and take care of their families. God is taking care of them now. I miss them something awful, but I'm still so thankful that they are with Him, enjoying the countless blessings God had stored up for them.

My friend used to say, "If you see anything good in me, it is God, not me." After she was diagnosed with cancer, she suffered from it for seven years, and it was so difficult watching her drift into God's loving arms. When she passed, she only weighed seventy-eight pounds because the cancer had slowly eaten her diseased body away.

After she died, I vowed that I'd never let anyone touch my life the way she did. The pain of losing her was too much to bear. I was still consumed with grief when my mother fell ill. My mother had always been there for me, and I couldn't fathom a world without her in it.

After my mother passed, I only wanted to be left alone. The gaping hole in my life from the absence of my friend and my mother left me tormented. In addition, I developed painful kidney stones and had surgery to remove the stones. But even after coming home from the hospital, I endured horrible pain. I actually laid on the floor for nearly two and a half weeks, not caring whether I lived or died, for I had already faced so much.

Just when I was about to give up completely and let my mental anguish overtake all of my will to live, a new person stepped into my life—a person who acted as the hands, feet, and eyes of God. It began with a few texts. *How are you? Anything I can do for you today?*

One day, I received a text that said, *I left you something in your mailbox.* I struggled to get up off the floor, but I made it out to the mailbox to discover a simple cup of potato soup.

Since I had been in such pain and sickness, my stomach had shrunk, and I was not hungry at all, but I guess God touched my heart to take a bite, and when I did, I realized just how good that soup was. After that cup of soup, I slowly began to get my strength back.

For the next three months, my new friend showered me with Christian love, muffins, soups, corn casseroles, vitamins, and, most importantly, prayers. And, eventually, I recovered—I climbed out of that deep, dark hole in which I had fallen.

I still miss the people who have gone before me. I always will. Of course, I have my memories, but they are never the same as the real deal. But I thank God for sending me someone when I needed it the most.

| 29 |

THOSE UGLY OLD GREEN SHOES

Therefore thou art inexcusable, O man, whosoever thou art that judgest:for wherein thou judgest another, thou condemnest thyself; for thou that judgest doest the same things.

Romans 2:1

A few months after my mother passed, I started going to my old country church again. My mom had recently moved her membership back there before she had passed and had tried to get me to do the same. So, I finally did.

When I entered the sanctuary, I spotted a nice, well-dressed lady who had lived in my neighborhood years ago. She was sitting on the back seat. She had moved off when she was younger but had returned to her old home place. Well, every Sunday morning, this lady would smile at me when I came out of the Sunday school room.

Eventually, we started talking to one another after church, and one Sunday, I mentioned that I'd be glad to come help her at her chicken houses. To be honest, I had become weary of staying at home by myself all day long, and I longed to get out of the house that my mom had passed in—at least for a day.

Unfortunately, I had torn both my rotary cuffs, and the sweet lady knew that helping her with her chicken houses required decent health in the shoulder areas so she thanked me for my offer but told me that I'd better wait until I had healed more.

Then, one miraculous Sunday, she invited me over to watch them process the eggs—they'd place the eggs in a container and then onto a cart to be wheeled into another room.

By then, I had *chickened* out and decided to stay in the routine and comfort of my home. But she continued to ask. In fact, you might say she insisted.

So, eventually, I gave in and decided to go. Arriving on her farm, she met me at the door with a grin from ear to ear. I looked her up and down and thought, *Where on earth is that clean-cut woman I've been talking to at church every Sunday morning.*

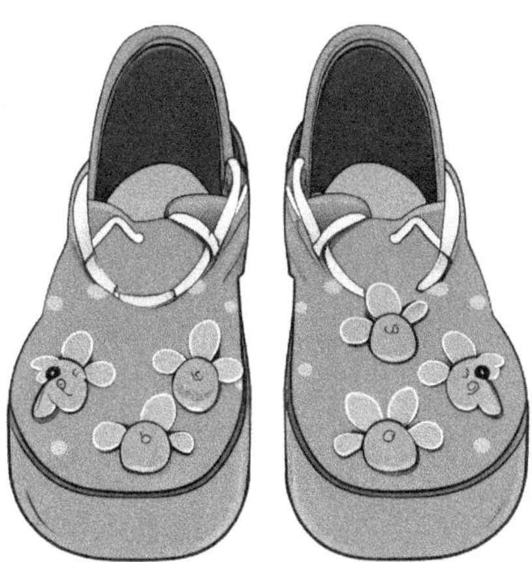

This woman had on a cap with her hair in a ponytail, and she had on a black, worn shirt with bleach stains all over it. Her black pants had little balls of lint stuck to them from so much washing, and when my eyes reached her feet, I gasped. Her shoes were ugly, old green clogs with bunny rabbits and carrots on them. To top it off, they were as dirty as could be.

I barely recognized her! The only thing I recognized was the bright Christian smile she always wore. After the shock wore off, I realized that she was dressed like that to work in the chicken house... which requires a wardrobe that you don't mind getting dirty.

The longer I stayed at her farm, the more I enjoyed it. In fact, I *needed* that time. After that, I began to go almost every day...then twice a day. She and I became very close. We told each other our problems without fear that they would be repeated. We asked each other about opinions on different subjects. We even had our Bible study together. Eventually, we started doing small deeds of kindness for the elderly and the sick in our community.

On one of our visits to an elderly woman's house, my friend wore her ugly, old green shoes, and the elderly lady asked her why she was wearing such hideous shoes.

My friend simply laughed and said, "I think they give me character."

We became closer and closer, and though I never did get quite used to those ugly old shoes, we did begin to serve God by serving others, which was very special.

I still chuckle, thinking about those old ugly green shoes and how God used them to bring another person into my life that would help me grow closer to Him.

| **30** |

SPECIAL MEMORIES OF GRANNY DOT

To everything there is a season, and a time to every purpose under the heaven; A time to be born, and a time to die; a time to plant, and a time to pluck up that which is planted; A time to kill, and a time to heal; a time to break down, and a time to build up; A time to weep, and a time to laugh; a time to mourn, and a time to dance; A time to cast away stones, and a time to gather stones together; a time to embrace, and a time to refrain from embracing. A time to get, and a time to lose; a time to keep, and a time to cast away; A time to rend, and a time to sew; a time to keep silence, and a time to speak; A time to love, and a time to "hate; a time of war; and a time of peace.

Ecclesiastes 3:1-8

The Bible states that for everything, there is a season… a time for everything. In farming, this is also true. Growing up, I can remember we would plant the seeds in the ground in spring. In the summer, we would work that which we had planted. In the fall, we would harvest what we had planted. In the winter, we would do other jobs that had to be done… like killing the hogs… and reflecting on what we had accomplished that planting season and planning for the future planting season.

I guess life is like that. We are born… which is like springtime. Then we grow and mature…which would be the summertime. In the fall, we retire and enjoy what we have accomplished throughout our lives. Then comes the dreaded winter… the time when we are too old to enjoy much… at a time when we sit around and reflect on our past.

I am now in the winter time of my life, and I'm asking God to show me how to give back to Him and how to correct my wrongs in life. I'm reflecting back on my past and trying my best to focus on the good things He has given me.

As I think back, I remember some awesome memories—but also some that are sad, some that are happy, some that are painful, and some that are just downright funny.

When I think back to my earlier years, I remember detesting going to school. I hated to leave my mama, and I wasn't sure if she would be home when I returned from school. I wanted so bad for her to protect me— and for me to protect her. But I was forced to go to school, anyway.

The first year I attended school, at recess, I would hide under the staircase and suck my thumb. Then, when I got back into the classroom, I'd just sit there and watch the clock. Even though I couldn't tell time, I knew when the hands of the clock got to a certain position, it would be time to get ready to go home to see my mom.

We had two recesses during the day. Mama would give me a dime to spend during one of those recesses, and she would give me a dollar for my lunch. I remember saving my money—not eating snacks or lunch—so that I could buy something for my mama. Paydays were Mama's favorite candy bar, so one day, I bought her eleven Paydays. I don't know if Mama ever ate all those candy bars, but I'd like to think my little sacrifice showed her how much I missed her.

At Christmas time, we got time off from school, and I was so glad. One Christmas, my grandfather had given each of us kids a few fireworks... mine being firecrackers because of my age. Still, I felt ten feet tall and bulletproof. I was lighting them all by myself with a firestick. I remember lighting a firecracker and was just about to throw it when Mama stepped out on the front porch and called me. I turned around and said, "What?"

About that time, the firecracker blew up in my hand. It sure did hurt, but I survived, and thinking back, I know I did the right thing by responding to Mama's call. Better my hand than my rear end.

Another memory that I often recall is the time my nephew and I went out hunting for a cow that had supposedly had a calf. At that time, my father had passed, and my mother was having some of her family, from out of state, visit her. My mother was so excited because she loved cooking for all her family, and she finally had a chance to do so.

So, while she was busy cooking, my nephew and I went to look for this calf in our go-cart. He was driving, and I was standing on the back, holding on for dear life. I was familiar with the territory, but he wasn't. He was laughing and having the time of his life, while I was praying. All of a sudden, I saw up ahead a ditch that was overgrown with weeds. The weeds were so tall, you couldn't really see the ditch, but I knew it was there.

I started screaming at the top of my lungs, "Ditch, ditch, ditch!"

He was grinning from ear to ear when we hit that ditch, wide open. The ditch was deeper than we were tall, and when we went down in it, the go-cart was standing on its nose, for although the ditch was deep, it wasn't wide. Smoke was coming out of the go-cart, and we were just lying there stunned.

My nephew was silent, and I thought maybe he had been knocked unconscious. My leg was hurting so bad, I thought that it was broken. I called him several times, and finally, he answered.

Luckily, we managed to crawl up and out of the ditch. Then, we reached down and drug the go-cart out. I was so afraid that it would catch on fire before we could get it turned back over because the gas was leaking. Thank the Lord that it didn't.

After we got the go-cart turned over, we flopped down on the ditch bank in awe. Just then, one of our neighbors drove down the road on his tractor. The road was several yards from us, and he waved at us. We waved back—but not for the same reason. We were trying to stop him, but he just kept waving and driving.

Any other time, Mama would have been checking on us because she was one of those moms who never let you out of her sight, but that day, I guess she was just so caught up in her company that she had plain forgotten about us.

I can't remember how we got home that day, but when I think back on it, I'm just happy that Mama was having a good time because she had so few occasions to enjoy herself.

Another sad memory often rushes into my mind. Mama's great-grandchildren always called her Granny Dot. Well, one day, my nephew was riding with his son in their truck. Their dog had recently died, and the son asked his dad if the dog had gone to heaven.

"You'll just have to ask the preacher about that," he told his son.

Then the son asked, "Isn't that where Granny Dot is?"

"Yes, son. Yes, it is," he replied.

"Well, why won't she come back and see us?" the child asked.

Of course, my nephew explained it the best he could to a five year old. "Once you die and go to heaven, it is so beautiful, even if you could, you still wouldn't want to come back because you love it there so much. And you are with God, who you love. And God loves you so much, so you just don't want to leave."

The child thought for a moment and said, "Well, Dad, you know I have saved up eight dollars, right?"

Thinking that his son was satisfied with the subject and had changed the subject, as children often do, he replied, "Yep, son. I know you've saved some money. That's a good thing. I'm proud of you."

Then, the boy blurted out, "Well would you tell Granny Dot she can have my eight dollars if she'll come back and see me?"

Life is filled with memories like this—ones that are both sad and funny at the same time. Thinking about the love that boy had for his Granny Dot makes me smile as much as imagining my mom dancing with Jesus.

ACKNOWLEDGEMENTS

I would like to thank Mary Snow, my sister in Christ. Not only does she believe we are to be the eyes, feet, and hands for Christ, but she always follows through on her beliefs and is always there to help others. She is a truly awesome and amazing person to be able to call a true friend.

I would like to say a special thanks to Jamie Gonzalez for all his patience and assistance with the computer help.

Thank you to Richard Westbrook, a truly gifted individual in more ways than one. Thanks for letting me use your amazing artwork.

I owe a special thanks to Betty Byrd for those awful ugly shoes she loves so dear.

Appreciation goes out to Kimberly Coghlan, my editor, who did an outstanding job when she had such little to work with.